Katie Clemons
LET'S CELEBRATE YOUR STORY

Love, MOM AND Me

A Mother & Daughter Keepsake Journal

sourcebooks
jabberwocky

TO MAUREEN AND MICHELLE, WHO
SHARE THE BEAUTY OF BEING A
DAUGHTER, SISTER, AND MOM WITH ME.

NIKLAS'S ART, AGE 4

Published by Sourcebooks Jabberwocky, an imprint of Sourcebooks, Inc.
P.O. Box 4410, Naperville, Illinois 60567–4410
(630) 961-3900
Fax: (630) 961–2168
sourcebooks.com

Originally published in 2016 in the United States of America by Katie Clemons LLC.

Source of Production: Versa Press, East Peoria, Illinois, USA
Date of Production: March 2022
Run Number: 5025123

Printed and bound in the United States of America.
VP 14 13 12

A Mom's Perspective

"Katie, what are you still doing in the bathroom?"

I swear my mom always knew when trouble was brewing. One of my best lessons came when I was about eleven years old.

"I'm not doing anything, Mom!" I shot back, frantically scooping up the confetti of hair clippings on the sink. I couldn't see a safe place to hide my evidence, so I tossed the blonde wad into the toilet and flushed.

"That doesn't sound like nothing."

I looked in the mirror and grimaced. So far, my new bangs—which were supposed to look adorable and bouncy like the model in the picture—resembled something a weed wacker might cough out. My friends were going to laugh, my brother and his cute buddies would tease me, and I'd never be able to leave home again. The harder I tried to fix my hair, the shorter and more ridiculous it became.

My mom leaned into the door and asked, "Are you okay in there? If you have anything you want to talk about, I'm right here."

"You don't get it, Mom. Everything's fine," I answered, trying not to do that choking sob thing. I jerked the medicine cabinet open and scanned the contents while tears blurred my vision. "I'm just trying out that new face wash you bought me."

Anyone else in the family wouldn't have given two seconds' notice to my tone. They'd have banged on the door to use the toilet or snoop around. But for whatever reason, my mom didn't push. She just said "okay" and returned to the living room.

Now that I'm a mom, I know how difficult it was for her to walk away. When my child is in distress, my primal reaction is to bust down the door and announce, "Let's talk about this right now. I'll fix everything!" I get so wrapped up in my own need to restore happiness that I forget: sometimes my child needs to learn how to overcome adversity without me.

Our hectic schedules make it easy to walk through the hall and completely miss a child's closed door. Keeping a journal helps us become both more aware and more confident. Writing prompts encourages us to slow down and be aware of what our children—and we!—are experiencing.

It's like watching clouds. Once we let ourselves lean into the grass, clouds transform from cotton balls in the sky to shapes and stories that dance and shift. We start seeing connections. You might see one story in the clouds; your daughter—looking through her lens of adolescence and varying life experiences—sees something different. Mother-daughter journaling lends you both the opportunity to recognize similarities and differences while openly discussing them.

I still remember searching for my mom that long-ago summer afternoon. She was sitting on a red-and-white gingham quilt spread across the lawn, sipping iced tea. "I did something bad," I told her.

She just patted the quilt beside her, inviting me to sit. I pulled the baseball cap off my head and showed her the porcupine my bangs had become. I wanted to cry all over again.

She set her tea down and smiled. "You know, I've been trying new things my whole life too. You never know what will happen if you don't pull out scissors and try."

Although I never shared a journal with my mom, moments like these are threads that connect me forever with her love.

I wrote this journal to encourage you and your daughter to share stories, daydreams, adventures, and to try and understand each other's point of view. A few prompts invite conversations on topics that may be difficult, but will bring you closer together.

These five guideposts will help you get the most from your storycatching time together.

❶ WRITE YOUR OWN RULES.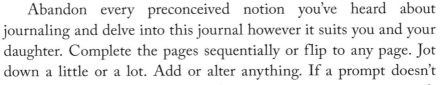

Abandon every preconceived notion you've heard about journaling and delve into this journal however it suits you and your daughter. Complete the pages sequentially or flip to any page. Jot down a little or a lot. Add or alter anything. If a prompt doesn't resonate with you, cross it out and create your own, or cover it with a drawing or photograph. Spread a quilt across the grass and answer questions together, or pass the book back and forth.

Your daughter's stories go on pages that begin "Dear Daughter" or "Daughter Writes." Corresponding "Dear Mom" and "Mom Writes" pages offer you an opportunity to respond or ignite another conversation. Intermixed throughout are spaces to write, doodle, and adhere mementos.

❷ Listen Completely.

The real joy of mother-daughter journaling starts when you read the words each other writes. It's like getting a peek inside one another's heads and hearts. Some entries may cover things you already know. Through others you might discover details, emotions, or entire stories that you weren't aware of—from her or yourself.

While you may feel tempted to lecture or point out her faults in these pages, try to understand what your daughter is really communicating. Does she want you to fix things for her, or does she actually just need you to lend an ear while she sorts things out?

Give her time and keep listening. When she chooses to share something difficult, you might feel inspired to respond immediately. But you can also walk away and ruminate on her words before you reply.

❸ Tell Complete Stories.

When we talk, it's easy to get caught up in worrying about what we perceive other people will think or say. Use this journal to focus on telling your own perspective and describing what you see and how you feel.

The goal isn't perfection—in life or these pages—because a messy journal is infinitely better than an empty one. I compose run-on sentences that fill half a page. Words get crossed out or written on top of each other. I'm certain I'll never be able to spell a single French word correctly (hors d'oeuvre?), and inevitably my words slowly fade as the pen I'm using runs out of ink. But I keep going, and I want you to, as well.

❹ ENJOY YOURSELVES.

As you write, also think of this journal as a place to play. Express yourselves on the pages in all kinds of ways: Jot an abundance of *xoxo*'s. Experiment with pens and stickers. Emphasize words by underlining or coloring them in. Write in all caps. Draw speech bubbles. Note thoughts and add arrows in the margins. Use glue or double-sided tape to adhere photographs, screenshots, notes, and anything else that encapsulates your life right now.

❺ GO BEYOND THESE PAGES.

Your mother-daughter journaling experience only begins in this book. Join me for exclusive *Love, Mom and Me* resources, including unexpected ways to swap top-secret messages in this book, creative journal-worthy projects your daughter will love, and examples from my own diaries on:

katieclemons.com/a/95D6

Want to tell me how your journal is coming together? Email **howdy@ katieclemons.com** (I answer all my mail) or join me on social media **@katierclemons, #katieclemonsjournals,** and **#lovemomandme.**

Imagine opening this journal in ten or twenty years or giving it to your grown daughter. You'll see pages filled with stories and perspectives, photographs, youthful penmanship recording both phrases you haven't heard in years and moments you'd nearly forgotten about, and best of all...reminders of how much you love each other.

YOU'RE A WONDERFUL MOM. Grab a blanket, spread it beneath the clouds, and... Let's celebrate your story! ♡Katie

YOU are the end OF MY RAINBOW

Here's a photograph or drawing of

YOU  ME

HELLO ♡ **WORLD!**

Our full names are

_____

_____

We call each other

_____

_____

We sign our names like this

_____

_____

We are _____ and _____ years old.

TODAY, WE BEGIN THIS JOURNAL!

Date_____

OUR JOURNAL
GUIDELINES

1 Is our journal top secret or can anyone else look inside?

2 If someone finds this journal, they should

☐ Return it

☐ Complete it

☐ Destroy it

☐ Share pages online

☐ Hide it in _____

☐ Sell it for $ _____

☐ Turn it into a _____ movie

3 Do we have to answer prompts in numerical order?

☐ Yes   ☐ No

4 Our top focus(es) in this journal will be to

☐ Express our thoughts

☐ Use perfect grammar

☐ Capture memories

☐ Skip our responsibilities such as _____ _____ in order to write

☐ _____

☐ _____

5 How much time do we have to write before passing our journal back to one another?

6 What could we do if we need more space to write?

7 Is there a specific date when this journal must be complete?

8 How do we pass our journal back and forth?

9 How should we tell each other which page to turn to?

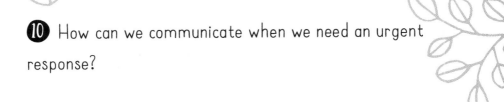

10 How can we communicate when we need an urgent response?

11 Are there other guidelines we should establish for our journal?

DEAR **MOM,**

What's something I do that makes you smile?

MOM WRITES

DEAR **DaughteR,**

What's something I do that makes you smile?

TIME FOR
A HUG!

you & me

We feel cozy when we wear

MOM

DAUGHTER

We feel powerful when we wear

MOM

DAUGHTER

We feel most like ourselves when we wear

MOM

DAUGHTER

WE WRITE

Daughter ❀ WRITES

Mom, the first thing you say to me in the morning is

The last thing you say to me before bed is

MOM ❀ WRITES

Daughter, the first thing you say to me in the morning is

The last thing you say to me before bed is

DEAR Daughter,

What are three of your most amazing accomplishments?

1

2

3

Is there another goal you want to achieve?

DEAR **MOM,**

What are your thoughts on what I wrote
about my achievements?

Do you think I can accomplish my goal?

DAUGHTER WRITES

Our family

Our community

Outside our house

Inside our house

MOM WRITES

Our family

Our community

Outside our house

Inside our house

WONDERFUL THINGS WE'VE DONE
TOGETHER

❶ _____

_____

_____

_____

_____

❷ _____

_____

_____

_____

❸ _____

_____

_____

_____

❹ _____

_____

_____

_____

WE WRITE

EXCITING THINGS WE STILL NEED TO DO
TOGETHER

1 _____

_____

_____

_____

_____

2 _____

_____

_____

_____

_____

3 _____

_____

_____

_____

_____

4 _____

_____

_____

_____

_____

DAUGHTER  WRITES

Mom, you are beautiful inside and out because

1

2

3

4

5

Here's a picture of you,

MY _____ MOM.

MOM  WRITES

Daughter, you are beautiful inside and out because

1

2

3

4

5

Here's a picture of you,

MY _____ DAUGHTER.

DaughTer WRITES

I look forward to the holiday season because

_____

_____

_____

_____

One of my favorite traditions is

_____

_____

_____

_____

I remember one time when

_____

_____

_____

_____

_____

Our house looks like

Our house smells like

People who make the season magical

I love these food traditions

MOM WRITES

When I was growing up, I remember looking forward to the holiday season because

_____

_____

_____

_____

One of my favorite traditions was

_____

_____

_____

I remember one time when

_____

_____

_____

_____

Our house looked like

Our house smelled like

People who made the season magical

I still cherish the memory of these foods

DEAR Daughter,

Tell me about a time you did something kind
for someone else even though you didn't have to.

AWESOME SPOT
TO DRAW.

HIGH FIVE!

Why did you do it?

How did it make you feel?

DEAR MOM,

What are your thoughts on kindness?

GREAT SPOT TO DOODLE.

MOM WRITES

Do you have a story of when you saw me being nice?

DEAR Daughter,

Which school subject is difficult for you?

Why do you think it's so hard?

How can I help make it easier?

DRAW HOW
YOU FEEL
ABOUT IT.

DEAR **MOM,**

What are your thoughts on what I wrote about school?

PERFECT TIME FOR A HUG

MOM WRITES

Which subject did you struggle with
when you were my age?

How does knowing that subject help your life today?

you & me

Three things that make us laugh out loud

> DAUGHTER

> MOM

WE WRITE

you & me

Our excited faces

MOM

DAUGHTER

Our frustrated faces

MOM

DAUGHTER

Our silly faces

MOM

DAUGHTER

DEAR MOM,

What were you like when you were my age?
What was your life like?

Date

DEAR Daughter,

How is your life different from
and similar to when I was a kid?

you ❤ me

We love this color

MOM

DAUGHTER

We love this texture

MOM

DAUGHTER

We love this pattern

MOM

DAUGHTER

WE WRITE

Daughter, I know you love me so much because

MOM WRITES

DAUGHTER WRITES

Mom, I know you love me so much because

DEAR MOM,

Tell me about your mom. What was she like when you were young? What do you admire about her now?

DEAR Daughter,

Tell me what you know and admire about your grandma.

DEAR **MOM,**

Tell me what you remember about your grandma.
What are some of your favorite memories of her?

DEAR **Daughter,**

What do you think about your great grandma
and the life she lived?

MOM  WRITES

Daughter, when you're _____ years old like I am now,
make sure you take time for yourself to

_____

_____

_____

_____

DAUGHTER WRITES

Mom, when I'm _____ years old like you are now,
make sure you take time for yourself to

_____

_____

_____

_____

MOM WRITES

Daughter, let me trace your hand here.

DaUGHteR WRITES

Mom, let me trace your hand here.

MOM WRITES

My typical weekday

6:00

7:00

8:00

9:00

10:00

11:00

NOON

1:00

2:00

3:00

4:00

5:00

6:00

7:00

8:00

9:00

10:00

DaughteR WRITES

My typical weekday

6:00 ....

7:00 ....

8:00 ....

9:00 ....

10:00 ....

11:00 ....

NOON ....

1:00 ....

2:00 ....

3:00 ....

4:00 ....

5:00 ....

6:00 ....

7:00 ....

8:00 ....

9:00 ....

10:00 ....

you ♥ me

The bravest woman we know

MOM

DAUGHTER

The most compassionate woman we know

MOM

DAUGHTER

The happiest woman we know

MOM

DAUGHTER

DAUGHTER ♡ WRITES

Mom, I want you to know it's
okay to ask for help when

MOM ♡ WRITES

Daughter, I want you to know it's
okay to ask for help when

DEAR **DAUGHTER,**

Tell me the story of

_____

_____

_____

DEAR **MOM,**

Why do you enjoy spending time with friends?

Which traits do you value in a friend?

What are things you don't want in friendship?

COOL!

How do you try to be a good friend?

Tell me about your closest friends when you were my age.

Are you still in touch? Why?

Show me a picture from when you were young.

DEAR **DauGHter,**

Why do you enjoy spending time with friends?

Which traits do you value in a friend?

What are things you don't want in friendship?

How do you try to be a good friend?

Tell me about your closest friends.

Show me a picture.

MOM WRITES

My favorite **HOLIDAY** is

because _____

_____

_____

_____

_____

_____

Here's us **CELEBRATING!**

DAUGHTER WRITES

My favorite HOLIDAY is

because _____

_____

_____

_____

_____

_____

Here's us CELEBRATING!

you & me

A woman we admire

MOM

DAUGHTER

A woman we trust

MOM

DAUGHTER

A woman we love

MOM

DAUGHTER

Here's a picture of
you & me
doing something we love.

Daughter WRITES

I'm getting excited about

_____

_____

I am curious about

_____

_____

I feel guilty for

_____

_____

I feel lonely when

_____

_____

I am angry about

_____

_____

I am worried because

_____

_____

I am grateful for

_____

_____

I'm ashamed of

_____

_____

I feel so happy when

_____

_____

I'm wondering when

_____

_____

I'm hopeful that

_____

_____

DEAR _____,

I have a question I want to ask you

_____

_____

_____

WE WRITE

Date

Date

DEAR MOM,

Tell me about a special gift I made you
when I was younger. Do you still have it?

Could you draw a picture?

DEAR Daughter,

What kinds of things do you enjoy creating now?

Could you draw a picture?

DEAR **MOM,**

Tell me about the first time you held me.

DAUGHTER WRITES

Mom,
thank you for

MOM WRITES

Daughter,
thank you for

DEAR **Daughter,**

What are four things you secretly wish you could do?

1

2

3

4

Daughter WRITES

DEAR MOM,

What do you think about the four things I wrote?

Was there anything you wished
you could do and then you did it?

DEAR Daughter,

Do you think women are treated equal to men?

Is this topic important?

Do you think there are ways our society could change?

DEAR **MOM,**

What do you think about what I wrote?

_____

_____

_____

_____

_____

Do you believe men and women are treated equally?

_____

_____

_____

_____

How do you think our society can improve?

_____

_____

_____

_____

DEAR **Daughter,**

I have a question for you

_____

_____

_____

DEAR MOM,

Tell me a story about when I was little.

TIME TO SAY
"I LOVE YOU."

DEAR **DaughteR,**

Describe how we celebrate your birthday.

Which tradition do you love most?

Tell me a favorite birthday memory.

DEAR **MOM,**

Describe how you celebrated your birthday when you were a kid.

Which tradition did you love most?

Tell me a favorite birthday memory.

 you & me

If we had the whole day to spend together

DAUGHTER

MOM

 you & me

Right now we're reading

MOM

Daughter

We're supposed to be

MOM

Daughter

We're looking forward to

MOM

Daughter

DEAR **MOM,**

Tell me about someone you admired
when you were young.

Who inspires you today?

Why is it important to have people you look up to?

DEAR Daughter,

Tell me about someone you admire.
Why do you admire him or her?

How are you similar to that person?

How can you be more like that person?

Why is it important to have people you look up to?

DEAR **MOM,**

What are three of your proudest accomplishments?

1

2

3

Is there another goal you want to achieve?

DEAR Daughter,

What do you think about the achievements I recorded?

Do you think I can accomplish my goal?

DEAR **MOM,**

What are some of your favorite parts of being a parent?

NICE SPOT
TO DOODLE.

Date

DEAR Daughter,

What do you think about what I wrote on motherhood?

Do you think you want to be a parent some day?

DEAR **MOM,**

Do you vote?

What do you think makes a good candidate?

DEAR Daughter,

Do you have questions about becoming a woman?

What are you excited about?

Is there anything you're nervous about?

Date

How do you feel about your body right now?

When are you confident about your body?

Do you ever feel uncomfortable about your appearance?

DEAR **MOM,**

What do you think about what I wrote?

Have you ever felt uncomfortable about your body?

When do you feel confident about your body?

Do you have any suggestions to help me become more comfortable or confident?

Tell me what you love about being a woman.

Daughter ❀ WRITES

If I knew I could never fail, I would

_____
_____
_____
_____
_____
_____
_____

MOM ❀ WRITES

Here's what I know about following your dreams

_____
_____
_____
_____
_____
_____
_____

 you & me

Our favorite leisurely breakfast

MOM

DAUGHTER

Our tastiest weekday lunch

MOM

DAUGHTER

Our most-dreaded dinner

MOM

DAUGHTER

MOM WRITES

Daughter, I always hear you say these expressions

Daughter WRITES

Mom, I always hear you say these expressions

DEAR MOM,

Tell me about an older relative that
I didn't get to know well.

ADD MEMORIES
AROUND THE
PICTURE FRAME.

DEAR **DaugHteR,**

What sport do you enjoy?

What do you like about it?

How do you feel when you're doing it?

DEAR **MOM,**

What are your thoughts on sports
and what I just wrote?

Did you play any sports when you were my age?

Did you enjoy them?

DEAR Daughter,

Is there anything you wish you could change about yourself or your life?

What would you never change?

DEAR MOM,

When you were my age,
what did you want to change about yourself?

_____

_____

_____

_____

Did you try to do anything about it?

_____

_____

_____

_____

How do you feel about it now?

_____

_____

_____

_____

you ♥ me

We constantly say

MOM

DAUGHTER

We consistently forget

MOM

DAUGHTER

We always laugh together when

MOM

DAUGHTER

WE WRITE

DAUGHTER WRITES

Mom,
I admire how you

MOM WRITES

Daughter,
I admire how you

DEAR **DAUGHTER,**

Do you remember a story from when you were little?

ADD YOUR
STORY
DOODLES HERE.

MOM  WRITES

Daughter, I'm proud of you because

I would describe you as a person who

One thing you always tell me is

You're really good at

I'm glad you regularly take time to

You have taught me

DAUGHTER ❀ WRITES

Mom, I'm proud of you because

I would describe you as a person who

One thing you always tell me is

You're really good at

I'm glad you regularly take time to

You have taught me

DEAR MOM,

When you were young,
what did you want to be when you grew up?

Did things go as planned?

What turned out better than you expected?

DEAR **Daughter,**

What do you want to be when you grow up?

Where would you like to live?

What kind of life would you like to have?

MOM WRITES

My absolute favorite

FOODS

1. _____
2. _____
3. _____
4. _____
5. _____

BOOKS

1. _____
2. _____
3. _____
4. _____
5. _____

MOVIES

1. _____
2. _____
3. _____
4. _____
5. _____

Daughter WRITES

My absolute favorite

FOODS

1. _____
2. _____
3. _____
4. _____
5. _____

BOOKS

1. _____
2. _____
3. _____
4. _____
5. _____

MOVIES

1. _____
2. _____
3. _____
4. _____
5. _____

DEAR **MOM,**

What was your favorite job before I was born?

How old were you? And how much did you get paid?

How did you travel to work?

What were your responsibilities?

Why did you like the job?

Tell me about a mistake you made or lesson you learned.

DEAR **DaughteR,**

What do you think about my favorite job?

Have you ever learned from a mistake
that you made?

What kind of jobs do you want
to experience?

Tell me about the kind of life you dream
of having when you're grown up.

MOM WRITES

THIS IS MY BEDROOM

I give my bedroom ☆☆☆☆☆ stars!

FILL IN FOR RATING.

IT USUALLY LOOKS LIKE

☐ a tornado hit

☐ a museum of oddities

☐ a paper explosion

☐ a cleaning commercial

☐ a gold mine

☐ a science experiment

☐ _____

That's because

_____

_____

_____

My favorite thing in here is

_____

When I was a kid, my room resembled a

_____

_____

_____

Daughter WRITES

THIS IS MY BEDROOM

I give my bedroom ☆ ☆ ☆ ☆ ☆ stars!

FILL IN FOR RATING

IT USUALLY LOOKS LIKE

- ☐ a tornado hit
- ☐ a museum of oddities
- ☐ a paper explosion
- ☐ a cleaning commercial
- ☐ a gold mine
- ☐ a science experiment
- ☐ _____

That's because

_____

_____

_____

My favorite thing in here is

_____

I like to be in my room when

_____

_____

_____

MOM WRITES

The money we have has enabled our family to

_____

_____

_____

These are times when money
doesn't matter to our family

_____

_____

_____

I think it's important to set aside money for

_____

_____

_____

I enjoy giving time or money to

_____

_____

_____

DaugHteR WRITES

The money we have has enabled our family to

_____

_____

_____

These are times when money doesn't matter to our family

_____

_____

_____

I think it's important to set aside money for

_____

_____

_____

I enjoy giving time or money to

_____

_____

_____

FUTURE PREDICTIONS

YOU AND ME IN _____ YEARS

Daughter, I anticipate you won't have to spend
any more time on

_____

_____

_____

You'll have more time to

_____

_____

You'll be really good at

For your birthday, you'll want

I'll probably give you

I'll have to start reminding you to

Most likely, you'll still be reminding me to

We'll continue to tell each other

DAUGHTER WRITES
FUTURE PREDICTIONS

YOU AND ME IN_____YEARS

Mom, I anticipate you won't have to spend
any more time on

_____
_____
_____

You'll have more time to

_____
_____

You'll be really good at

For your birthday, you'll want

I'll probably give you

I'll have to start reminding you to

Most likely, you'll still be reminding me to

We'll continue to tell each other

MOM WRITES

I always look forward to

SPRING

SUMMER

FALL

WINTER

DAUGHTER WRITES

I always look forward to

SPRING

SUMMER

FALL

WINTER

MOM WRITES

Here's a keepsake from my life right now

It's a

- ☐ ticket stub
- ☐ receipt
- ☐ wrapper
- ☐ newspaper clipping
- ☐ quote or poem
- ☐ list or note from my pocket
- ☐ photo or picture
- ☐ _____

I'm adding it to our journal because

DaughteR WRITES

Here's a keepsake from my life right now.

───▶ It's a ◀───

- ☐ ticket stub
- ☐ receipt
- ☐ wrapper
- ☐ newspaper clipping

- ☐ quote or poem
- ☐ list or note from my pocket
- ☐ photo or picture
- ☐ _____

I'm adding it to our journal because

you & me

People might guess we're related because

DAUGHTER

MOM

DEAR Daughter,

Tell me what else is on your mind.

Here's a picture of
you ♥ me

being _____.

DEAR Daughter.

HOORAY! We've reached the end of this journal. What did you enjoy about writing together?

How should we celebrate our journal's completion?

What will we do with our journal?

What do you want to do together next?

LET'S CELEBRATE YOUR STORY!

I believe that your story is one of the most meaningful gifts you can give yourself and the people you love. Thank you for entrusting me and this journal with your adventures. If you loved writing in these pages, let's celebrate more of your story with my other books. They're just as empowering and, well, awesome!

♡ Katie

BETWEEN MOM AND ME: A Mother & Son Keepsake Journal

BETWEEN DAD AND ME: A Father & Son Keepsake Journal

LOVE, DAD AND ME: A Father & Daughter Keepsake Journal

BETWEEN GRANDMA AND ME: A Grandmother & Grandson Keepsake Journal

LOVE, GRANDMA AND ME: A Grandmother & Granddaughter Keepsake Journal

LOVE BETWEEN GRANDPA AND ME: A Grandfather & Grandchild Keepsake

WE ARE SO THANKFUL: A Shared Gratitude Journal

TIME CAPSULE: A Seriously Awesome Journal

SPREAD YOUR WINGS: A Self-Discovery Journal

AWAITING YOU: A Pregnancy Journal

TAKE TIME: A Mother's Journal

HERE I GO: A Travel Journal

OUR PRAYER JOURNAL: Celebrating Our Christian Faith Together

DISCOVER EVEN MORE KATIE CLEMONS
JOURNALS AT KATIECLEMONS.COM!